FENG SHUI

DOS & TABOOS

for FINANCIAL SUCCE$$

Also by Angi Ma Wong

Feng Shui Dos & Taboos
Feng Shui Dos & Taboos for Love

❊ ❊ ❊

Hay House Titles of Related Interest

Books
The Abundance Book, by John Randolph Price
Feng Shui for the Soul, by Denise Linn
Home Design with Feng Shui A–Z, by Terah Kathryn Collins
The Little Money Bible, by Stuart Wilde
Space Clearing A–Z, by Denise Linn
The Western Guide to Feng Shui, by Terah Kathryn Collins
The Western Guide to Feng Shui for Prosperity,
by Terah Kathryn Collins
The Western Guide to Feng Shui: Room by Room,
by Terah Kathryn Collins

Card Decks
Feng Shui Personal Paradise Cards,
by Terah Kathryn Collins
I Can Do It® Cards: Affirmations for Wealth, by Louise L. Hay
Money Cards, by Suze Orman

❊ ❊ ❊

All of the above titles are available at your local bookstore,
or may be ordered by calling Hay House at (800) 654-5126.

ANGI MA WONG

FENG SHUI

DOS & TABOOS

for FINANCIAL SUCCE$$

LIFE
Styles

Hay House, Inc.
Carlsbad, California • Sydney, Australia • London, U.K.
Canada • Hong Kong

Published and distributed in the United States by: Hay House, Inc., P.O. Box 5100, Carlsbad, CA 92018-5100 • *Phone:* (760) 431-7695 or (800) 654-5126 • *Fax:* (760) 431-6948 or (800) 650-5115 • www.hayhouse.com • **Published and distributed in Australia by:** Hay House Australia Ltd., 18/36 Ralph St., Alexandria NSW 2015 • *Phone:* 612-9669-4299 • *Fax:* 612-9669-4144 • www.hayhouse.com.au • **Published and Distributed in the United Kingdom by:** Hay House UK, Ltd. • Unit 202, Canalot Studios • 222 Kensal Rd., London W10 5BN • *Phone:* 44-20-8962-1230 • *Fax:* 44-20-8962-1250 • www.hayhouse.co.uk • **Distributed in Canada by:** Raincoast • 9050 Shaughnessy St., Vancouver, B.C. V6P 6E5 • *Phone:* (604) 323-7100 • *Fax:* (604) 323-2600

Editorial supervision: Jill Kramer • *Cover design:* Christy Salinas
Interior design: Amy Gingery

ISBN 1-4019-0100-X

06 05 04 03   4 3 2 1
1st printing, August 2003

Printed in Canada

CONTENTS

A PERSONAL MESSAGE

My sincere thanks go to all my readers for making *Feng Shui Dos & Taboos* (both the original and gift-book versions) and *Feng Shui Dos & Taboos for Love* such terrific successes. Because you love the easy-to-read format of my chunky little books, here's another one for you!

It's my pleasure to continue to bring you new information and tools to help you further your feng shui knowledge and strengthen efforts to transform your life. If you're a hands-on kind of person, you'll find all three of my user-friendly, goof-proof tools—*Feng Shui Desk for Success Tool Kit, Feng Shui Room-by-Room Home Design Kit,* and *Feng Shui Garden Design Kit* (all of which may be purchased at my Website: **www.FengShuiLady.com**)—the perfect companions to the book you currently hold in your hands. Open up any of the imprinted kits (which come complete with compasses), and you can immediately start setting up your home, workspace, and/or outdoor environment according to feng shui.

To those of us of Chinese heritage, feng shui is an integral part of our lives. It was and still is commonplace in Hong Kong, Singapore, Taiwan, and in Chinese communities around the world to consult feng shui masters before burying the dead; buying, leasing, or renting property; opening a business; or building a temple or any other structure.

As a traditional, classically trained feng shui consultant, I'm passionate about maintaining excellence as well as cultural integrity by practicing this art as close to its (and my) Chinese roots as I can. As you join me in this mission, I

A PERSONAL MESSAGE

extend to you my heartfelt thanks and grati-
tude. May your pure hearts, integrity, and strong
intentions bring you the blessings of good health,
lasting and rewarding relationships, personal
growth, and financial abundance.

Best wishes,
Angi Ma Wong

Websites: **www.FengShuiLady.com**
             www.AsianConnections.com

E-mail: **angi@FengShuiLady.com**

INTRODUCTION

My seemingly healthy 89-year-old father, Shui Tong Ma, died suddenly in his sleep on November 20, 1999. It was up to Mom, my brother, and me to handle all the details concerning his funeral and burial. While Dad had already chosen a cemetery in the town where he and Mom had retired 14 years previously, the decision regarding his gravesite was left up to us.

As the oldest child and the most knowledgeable about feng shui, I took on the responsibility of finding the optimal final resting place for Dad to show my love and respect for this wonderful, caring man who profoundly influenced my life and made me the person I am. Like countless Chinese before me, I believed that if I took care in honoring him with a location that had the best possible feng shui, he'd take care of my mother and brother and me, because we're connected in spirit forever.

The plot we decided on was ideal, and "feng shui compliant." It was in the classic horseshoe configuration—that is, the plot was on an incline with a tall mountain behind it, two smaller ones on each side in front of it, and a wide view in the front of my parents' home about two miles away. Visibility was impressive at about 30 miles, encompassing vegetable fields in the foreground, a highway in the distance (representing flowing water), the bleachers of the high school football field beyond, and a range of mountains. A refreshing breeze and birds singing in the nearby trees made the location a beautiful and peaceful spot that comforted me each time I went to pay my respects to Dad.

Within two months of his funeral, my business skyrocketed and has remained extremely successful, which I attribute to good feng shui. But I knew that my actions, words, and deeds (which showed my father continual respect, compassion, love, and affection) *while he was alive* did more for my personal feng shui than all the changes I ever could have made to his grave, or to my home or workplace.

Chinese emperors who wanted to ensure a lengthy reign in their families' dynasties made choosing their own gravesites a top priority soon after they came into power. And Chinese towns were planned to take advantage of the two critical characteristics of healthy human settlements: fresh air and clean water—in short, good *feng* (wind) and good *shui* (water).

Feng shui shares the same three fundamental concepts as traditional Chinese medicine (TCM) does. Chi gong, tai chi, acupuncture, acupressure, martial arts, herbs, and tonics are all related to this 4,000-year-old holistic philosophy of living in harmony and balance with the cycles and rhythms of nature, the earth, and the universe. While the West is predisposed to the theme of "*veni, vidi, vici* (I came, I saw, I conquered)," the East has always had a reverence and healthy respect for nature and has sought to coexist with it.

The **first** concept that feng shui shares with all of these pursuits is the flow of *chi*—the universal, cosmic energy that surrounds and connects us all. Beneficial chi always flows in wavy or curved lines, like the wind and water in nature. Negative energy, which always travels in straight paths, is called *sha chi* (or "killing energy") because there are very few perfectly long, straight lines in nature. The movement of chi is essential to both the interior environment of our bodies as well as to the exterior environment in which we exist, both indoors and out.

The **second** concept of feng shui is that of harmony and balance. To the Chinese, this is represented by the tai chi symbol, featuring the teardrop-shaped halves known as *yin* and *yang*. Yin, meaning "dark," is the feminine half: soft, negative, passive, and nurturing. Yang means "light," and it's the masculine half: hard, positive, and aggressive. Yin and yang are *not* opposites of each other; rather, they're halves of a whole. In the yin side, there's a dot of the yang, and in the yang half, there's a dot of the yin, for the Chinese realized that everything male still had a trace of the female within, and the female had a bit of the male as well. Moreover, when yin decreases, yang increases, and vice versa—just like night becoming day and day becoming night—duplicating the perpetual cycle of birth and life in nature and the universe.

The S curve that separates the two dualities isn't fixed, but shifts according to the proportion

Figure A –
The Tai Chi Symbol

of yin to yang, yang to yin. To feel and become centered, we achieve balance by living through our actions, thoughts, food, exercise, meditation, and so on. In feng shui, such balance is reached through colors, textures, light, walls, windows, doors, and other architectural and design features in a home or office, as well as the forces of nature.

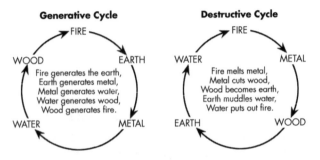

Figure B – The Generative and Destructive Element Cycles

The **third** major idea in both feng shui and TCM is that of the five elements: wood, fire, earth, metal, and water. They relate to each other in two different ways, generative and destructive. In the generative relationship, one element is the source for the next; while in the destructive cycle, an element can destroy another. There's nothing superstitious or metaphysical about these relationships—in fact, you can see them at work in nature.

In TCM, each element is associated with various organs and parts of the human body, and they relate in both a generative and a destructive manner. Poor health, illness, and death are believed to be caused by an imbalance of the elements or an obstruction of chi flow within one's body.

Five Components of Destiny

The Chinese believe that feng shui is only one of the five components that make up our destinies. The other four are fate, luck, charity, and education.

Fate represents all the circumstances of our birth, which includes time, family, ethnicity, status, socioeconomic circumstances, and so forth. Luck consists of three different kinds: heaven, pure, and man-made. Good heaven luck puts you before or after a terrible accident at a busy intersection; bad heaven luck places you *in* that accident. Pure luck is exactly that—the woman from the Philippines who called her relatives in California to buy her one lottery ticket and won several million dollars certainly had pure luck. Man-made luck is taking part in creating your own opportunities in order to bring you good fortune. Then comes feng shui, the ancient Chinese environmental system of aligning human energies with that of nature and the universe. Fourth is charity and philanthropy: your doing good deeds and sending out positive energy into the universe, or reaping what you sow. I contend that with money or love, the more you give, the more you receive . . . and often in unexpected and surprising ways. Last, but not least, is self-cultivation and education—we should all be constantly developing personally, professionally, physically, mentally, spiritually and emotionally. Remember what actress Helen Hayes said: "If you rest, you rust."

Schools of Feng Shui

It's been said that over time there have been more than 30 schools or forms of feng shui. But today, two schools have emerged as the most popular in the world: the traditional, classical Compass School and the Black Sect Tantric Tibetan Buddhist School. Both transpose the octagon called the *bagua* on various rooms to determine what to place where within a space, and both assign different aspects of one's life to the various areas of a room—but they do these things in dramatically different fashions. And while in the United States, Black Sect appears to have great appeal, in the rest of the world, Compass School rules!

Even though I'm a classically trained, traditional Compass School practitioner, I've been practicing, writing, and teaching an integrated form of feng shui for many years, so I'm happy to share that information with you in this book.

The Compass School

In the Compass School, which is more than 3,000 years old and practiced all over the world, a compass (Chinese or Western) is used to identify a space's magnetic North first, after which the remaining seven directions fit into place: North is always North in a room, office, or garden; South is always South, and so forth. The compass directions are fixed and constant, and the bagua map subsequently matches the nine zones formed by a grid placed over a space. Eight areas are associated with different aspects of one's life and are associated with the eight cardinal and secondary compass directions of N, NE, E, SE, S, SW, W, and NW, plus a center.

The following list explains the eight compass directions and what they represent in the Compass School:

- **North (N):** Career and business success; black; winter; water; metal element; tortoise; the number 1

- **Northeast (NE):** Love of learning; spiritual, intellectual, mental, and emotional growth; turquoise, blue, or green; winter becoming spring; fire; earth element; the number 8

- **East (E):** Family, harmony, health, and prosperity; new beginnings; green, black, or blue; spring; wood element; water; dragon; the number 3

- **Southeast (SE):** Wealth, prosperity, and abundance; green or purple; spring becoming summer; wood element; water; the number 4

- **South (S):** Fame and fortune; longevity; festivity and joy; red; summer; wood element; fire; bird; the number 9

- **Southwest (SW):** Love, marriage, mother, relationships, and spouse; teamwork; gold, yellow, red, pink, or white; summer becoming autumn; earth element; fire; the number 2

- **West (W):** Children; creativity; white or silver; autumn; metal element; earth; tiger; the number 7

- **Northwest:** Father; helpful people, mentors, and benefactors; interests outside the home; trade; travel; gray, white, or yellow; autumn becoming winter; metal element; earth; the number 6

Dir.	Color	Animal	No.	Element	Season
N	Black, blue	Tortoise	1	Water	Winter
NE	Turquoise		8	Earth	Winter to Spring
E	Green, blue	Dragon	3	Wood	Spring
SE	Green, purple		4	Wood	Spring to Summer
S	Red, purple	Phoenix	9	Fire	Summer
SW	Yellow, pink, red		2	Earth	Summer to Fall
W	White, metallic	Tiger	7	Metal	Fall
NW	Gray, metallic		6	Metal	Fall to Winter

Figure C – Compass School Directions

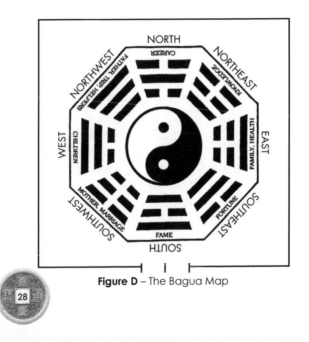

Figure D – The Bagua Map

The Black Sect School

The Black Sect Tantric Tibetan Buddhist School of feng shui has been popularized in the United States in the last two decades, although its roots trace back to Buddhism. This school doesn't need or use a compass at all. As in the Compass School, the bagua octagon governs certain aspects of one's life, but these are called "aspirations" or goals. What distinguishes this form of feng shui from others is that the bagua rotates, room by room, depending on where the main entrance is. For instance, the center of the wall where the main entrance is located is always the Career area.

The Black Sect School also relies greatly on its "Nine Cures": wind chimes and bells; crystals; mirrors; lights; plants and flowers; aquariums and fishbowls; moving or powered objects; heavy objects; and bamboo flutes.

The list below describes what each area of a room represents according to the Black Sect School:

- **Front Center** (at the entrance looking into the room): Career; black or white; fountains; water

- **Left Front:** Knowledge, self-development, and success; personal goals and health; blue, black, or green; books

- **Left Center:** Family and ancestors; health; blue or green; heirlooms; shrines; photos

- **Left Rear:** Wealth, prosperity, abundance, and material things of value; red, purple, blue, or green; fountains, aquariums, and fish; banners

- **Center Rear** (across from main entrance): Fame and fortune; red or green; candles and fireplaces; awards and diplomas

31

- **Right Rear:** Marriage, relationships, spouse, and romance; mother; yellow

- **Right Center:** Children and creativity; white; metal; arts and crafts, toys, and games

- **Right Front:** Friends and supportive and helpful people; travel; father; black, white, or gray; religious icons

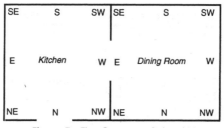

Figure E – The Compass School Map

Figure F – The Black Sect School Map

Take a moment to look at how different two adjoined rooms look from the perspectives of the Compass and Black Sect Schools as shown in the identical floor plans on the previous page. You've probably figured out that you can't mix these two forms of feng shui because where you place your enhancements will differ significantly from the Compass School to the Black Sect School.

Now take a few minutes to compare and understand the differences between these two popular forms of feng shui, and then choose the one that feels right for you. Whichever it is, be consistent and use common sense.

Using Feng Shui to Attract Wealth and Prosperity

By consulting the above, you can see where you should place items according to the two schools. Years ago, I created the acronym CANE to help friends and clients remember what to place where. The letters represent: (C)olor, (A)nimal symbol, (N)umber, and (E)lement. By putting the right CANEs in the right place, you'll stimulate the energy in that area.

Remember to practice feng shui with a pure heart and strong intentions. Gladly use this wonderful, ancient knowledge for your personal enrichment, but never harm anyone. In other words, it's acceptable to strengthen your financial position in life with feng shui, but using it to eliminate your competition in business, destroy another person's livelihood in order to advance your own, or succumb to greed, trickery, or theft creates bad karma and will surely backfire.

Even the most legendary of the world's tycoons kept things in their proper perspective:

"No man becomes rich unless he enriches others."
— ANDREW CARNEGIE

"It is in giving that we receive. We sow abundantly, we reap abundantly."
— CHOA KOK SU

I'm fond of saying that when it comes to money or love, the more you give, the more you gain. If you share your blessings with those less fortunate than you, you'll actually receive a gift yourself. And remember that there are many forms of wealth, not all of which can be seen in an impressive bank account, the ownership of real estate, or shares in Fortune 500 companies. *The emperor is rich,* an old Chinese proverb

37

reminds us, *but he cannot buy an extra day.* Good health and happiness are worth more than gold.

Chinese moguls and Western tycoons alike generally consult their feng shui advisors long before building or occupying a new office, thus ensuring their business's success. Then they stay put, establishing and developing a presence, reputation, and history at one location. As their companies grow, these wise men and women expand their workplaces cautiously, often eventually purchasing the very building that housed the office where they first made their fortune.

In evaluating the feng shui of a piece of property, there's a long list of characteristics to keep in mind, all of which depend on which school of feng shui you subscribe to. The following four attributes are what I consider the most significant considerations for an assessment, along with the three basic concepts of feng shui (chi, harmony, and balancing the five elements).

1. In both schools, *the shape of the land* is of primary importance, because it was present before any man-made structures were ever constructed. The earliest humans lived close to the earth, literally, in caves and under outcroppings of rocks long before pulling branches over themselves to provide shelter. But what do I mean by "the shape of the land"?

— Earlier I talked about placing my father's gravesite in the horseshoe configuration—this is also considered ideal and natural in buildings. For example, in an urban environment, tall buildings behind your own would serve as the "horseshoe's" protective back; in more rural areas, a stand of trees or a mound of dirt at least ten feet high would qualify.

— Your home or building should never be the tallest in the city (such as the World Trade Center towers in New York City were), or its arrogance and vulnerability will make it a target. But it shouldn't be dwarfed either; rather, it should fairly match its neighbors in size and style.

— And consider how the elements of the land relate to one another. For example, one might initially conclude that Manhattan has the right combination of elements. And yes, it is true that from the air, the island represents the earth element surrounded by the water element, which brings trade, commerce, and prosperity. However, upon closer inspection, the center (or core) of Manhattan Island is Central Park, which, with its size and lush vegetation, can only represent the wood element. When the park was conceived in the 1800s, it was supposed to block off the proliferation of encroaching skyscrapers, but by the early 1900s, it had become a symbol of the great divide between the yang (the wealthiest residents on Park Avenue) and the yin (those who lived in poverty and despair in Harlem). Now if you factor in your knowledge of the two relative cycles of the elements, you can see that Manhattan's earth element is destroyed by that of wood, just as the roots of a tree can wreck a sidewalk or those of a houseplant can break open a clay planter.

2. The plants and animals indigenous to the property should be taken into consideration. I always ask detailed questions with respect to whether a piece of property sustains life. Again, look at the presence of the wood element in Central Park: As people began to inhabit Manhattan, the natural flora and fauna of the park changed forever, as did the climate of the area—sea breezes and chi flow became obstructed by New York City's concrete jungle.

3. One shouldn't overlook or ignore the *historical or spiritual events* that have taken place on

a piece of land or in a building. There's a world of difference between a house in which a suicide, murder, or divorce has occurred compared to the "clean slate" of a new home that has no history. On the other hand, if you knew that all of the single women who lived in your new apartment went on to get married, or that the office you're moving into was vacated by a tremendously successful business that's now expanding, you probably wouldn't hesitate to sign a lease.

None of us can ever forget the tragedy that happened at the World Trade Center. Consequently, the site will always be remembered as a place of death and destruction and as a mass gravesite. From a feng shui perspective, it's imperative that the entire area be cleansed, purified, and blessed before any building takes place. My vision for this sacred ground is a single megastructure that integrates the activities of living, working, business, community, transportation, remembrance, and life. This will symbolize the soul and unity of the city as well as the nation, serving as a cultural and spiritual center. And why not let an eternal flame burn in the heart of the building (where a memorial and museum could be located) symbolizing perpetuality? But no matter what is eventually built there, the ground-breaking and dedication times and dates should be carefully calculated and adhered to so that the new building on that site enjoys a new life and longevity.

4. Last but not least, look at every *man-made structure* that encircles your home or office—roads and bridges; the shapes, colors, and sizes of the buildings surrounding you; and the lamp-posts, signage, locations of manholes . . . in short, nothing can be dismissed. Because man-made things aren't natural, they generally generate killing sha energy, so just be aware.

INTRODUCTION

As you practice feng shui, keep a journal or diary that records the things you did to attract prosperity, and the dates you did them. Follow up by recording the results.

In conclusion, remember the "3 Golden Rules of the Feng Shui Lady":

1. If it isn't broken, don't fix it. Ask yourself if you're happy, healthy, and prosperous: If the answers are yes, yes, and yes, then only fine-tune or make minor changes in your life. You don't want to make major overhauls and upset the blessings and good things you already have.

2. If you don't see it, it isn't there. Feng shui is a mental, practical, metaphysical, and spiritual process that uses a range of strategies—including assessment, addition, camouflage, removal, deflection, transformation, and protection.

3. Everything is fixable. Feng shui offers hope, empowerment, and a marvelous opportunity for taking charge and being proactive to change your life.

And now, enjoy this treasure trove of feng shui dos and taboos for enhancing prosperity and financial success in your life!

DOS & TABOOS

for FINANCIAL
SUCCE$$

Do use feng shui enhancements with restraint and good taste—in line with your imagination, style, and creativity. You don't want your home or business resembling a Chinese souvenir shop (unless it is one!).

Do accessorize your business with symbols of prosperity: gold coins, arrows, dragons, wish-fulfilling cows, and so forth.

Do elevate your

altar off the floor.

Don't put your altar in a

busy hallway or

room.

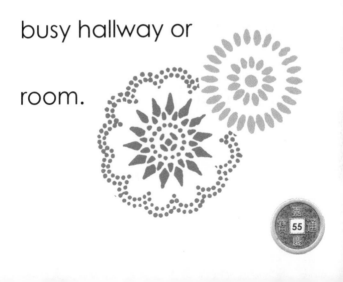

Do set your altar away from a bath-room or toilet.

Do keep your altar neat, clean, and free of clutter. Be sure to remove wilted flowers, dried fruit, and other stale offerings often.

Don't put a lucky three-legged prosperity toad on your altar table.

Do maintain lights or
candles on your altar.

Don't situate an altar to a deity close to your bed's pillow.

Do match figurines of animals to the elements of their compass directions: E or SE for wood, NW or W for metal, NE or SW for earth, N for water, and S for fire.

Do put a wish-fulfilling
cow in your office.

Do use artwork

with elephants

for long life and

high moral

values.

Don't adorn your space with images of foxes or coyotes, for they emanate much negative energy.

Do decorate with wood-carved

dragon figurines, as they

represent new beginnings.

Do keep a shed

snakeskin you find

as a symbol of riches

coming.

Don't create bad karma by killing snakes that happen onto your property. Catch and release them elsewhere instead.

Do take care of a stray dog if one shows up at your doorstep, for it represents good fortune coming to your home.

Don't introduce any antique funeral pieces from any country into your office decoration. This will bring in dark yin energy that might adversely affect your business.

Don't bring any antique

furnishings into your home

unless you cleanse its

energy first.

Don't keep antique bells in your home because they're rung at funerals.

Do put an aquarium in your office or home for career advancement and business growth.

Don't place an aquarium so that it faces a bathroom.

Do have your aquarium next to or facing the main entrance of your business.

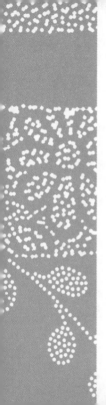

Don't put a fish tank in

your bathroom, or the

effects will be changed

from positive to negative.

Do maintain the fish, water, pumps, and tanks in good condition to keep the chi moving.

Don't set an aquarium

close to the ground, but

rather at waist height.

Do populate your tank with a single "prosperity fish"—the arowana—which moves like a metallic ribbon near the surface, and its gold or silver color represents metal coins.

Do keep an odd (yang) number of fish in your aquarium.

Don't worry if any
of your fish die—
it's believed that
they've absorbed
a calamity meant
for you.

Do accessorize your work

environment with

art that uplifts

and inspires you.

Don't decorate with any artwork that depicts weaponry, hunting, or dead people or animals.

Do put images and artwork

symbolizing wealth in your

place of business.

Don't hang art depicting battle scenes on land or sea in your office.

Do decorate with the symbol of the double carp to foster a successful union or business partnership.

Don't buy a rug with a dragon motif, for it's unlucky to step on these auspicious, mythical creatures.

Do bury your loved ones or their ashes in a location with great feng shui.

Don't store the ashes of pets or people in your bedroom.

Don't buy a house in which a bathroom is past the front line of the main entrance, for this represents the loss of wealth.

Don't choose a home with a bathroom situated on the second floor above the main entrance—this symbolizes calamity coming to the household.

Don't choose a residence that has a bathroom visible from the main entrance.

Do enclose your home bathrooms.

Don't live in a house in which

a bathroom is located in the

money-luck areas of S, SE, or E.

Don't situate any dragon figurines next to or in a bathroom or laundry room.

Don't spend a lot of time

or money decorating

your bathrooms.

Don't locate your cash register under a beam, stairway, or shelf; in other words, anything that would press energy down on it.

Do place a figurine of a rooster facing a row of beams in a room to prevent emotional or geographic separation from your family members.

Don't sit with your desk or chair directly under a beam or other ceiling protrusion, for this will push down on your energy.

Don't sleep in a bed that has a beam bisecting it either vertically or horizontally.

Don't put a statue of a deity under a shelf or beam in your home or business.

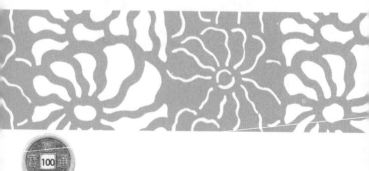

Do hang a grouping of
three Chinese coins tied
together with red ribbon
on your headboard on
the yang side (which,
when you're lying
down, is on the left
side) of the bed.

Don't position your bed behind a door.

Don't place your bed against the short wall of a sloped ceiling.

Don't have your feet pointing toward a door when you occupy your bed, as this position replicates that of the deceased being carried out of a home.

Do place a black onyx
ball under your bed
for protection.

Don't occupy a bed that receives the glare of car headlights—this strong, killing energy will disturb your chi and rest.

Do position your altar past the foot of your bed if your bedroom is the only room you have for it.

Do cleanse the energy in your bedroom several times a year by smudging, ringing bells, clapping, or other methods.

Don't use your bed-room for a family or TV room.

Do keep your room clutter-free

so that healthful, beneficial

chi can move freely around

the room and

your bed.

Don't install a

skylight in a

bedroom, especially

over a bed.

Do avoid putting any water elements in your bedroom, as they'll drain out your prosperity.

Don't hang dragon pictures in your bedroom—they're too yang and stimulating.

Do minimize the presence of live plants in your bedroom.

Don't set up your altar on your bed-room's nightstand.

Do take away as much

electronic gadgetry from your

bedroom as possible.

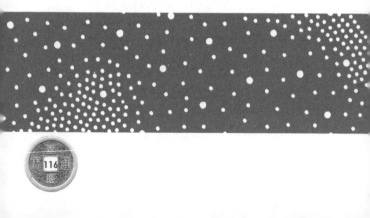

116

Do hang a string of tin-kling brass bells on a red ribbon or cord on the inside of your shop's door—unless it faces E or SE (both wood areas), as metal destroys wood.

Do hang an odd number of bells on the outside handle of your business to welcome customers in.

Don't bring bells
from either temples
or churches onto
your property, as
these have funeral
connotations.

Do ring a handbell in all the corners of your home to clear the air after a quarrel or negative occurrence.

Don't ever give the gift of a clock or bell to a Chinese friend or associate, for this is an unlucky symbol of death.

Do adorn your home or office with a pair of cranes to represent wealth and longevity.

Do decorate your business with a picture of an eagle or hawk in flight to symbolize unlimited potential and possibilities.

Do use images of a group of pheasants in your family business location, for they represent continuation.

Do own a pet bird
for prosperity.

Do choose a white bird such
as a cockatiel for a pet if you
were born in the fall.

Do own a green bird or fish if your birthday is during the spring.

127

Do keep a red

bird or fish if you

were born in the

summer.

128

Do own a black or blue bird or fish if you were born in the winter.

Do put your inspirational, sales, and marketing publications in the communications area of N.

Don't store too many books in your bedroom or office in plain sight. Keep them in closed bookcases or cabinets.

Do all the sweeping at your home or workplace (and put away the broom) before midnight of the Chinese New Year.

Don't vacuum or sweep in your home or office for two weeks following the first day of the Chinese New Year or you'll remove the good luck and fortune of the new year.

Do store your business's brooms, mops, buckets, and other cleaning accessories in a closed storage area.

Do use lots of candles

in the S to bring fame

and fortune to your

home.

Don't place any candles in the metal areas of W (creativity) or NW (helpers, benefactors, and mentors), as fire destroys metal.

136

Do keep candles or lights safely burning on your altar.

Don't position your cash register in the back of your shop; instead, place it against either side wall, close to the front, or in the center front.

138

Do install a mirror on both sides or behind your register or credit-card machine to "double" your business's money intake.

Don't put your cash register anywhere near rest rooms, since this represents money draining out.

140

Do dangle a round, sparkling crystal suspended by a red cord or ribbon over your cash register.

Do anchor an amethyst crystal or geode on top of your cash register.

Don't hang or store cigarettes, candy, snacks, or other displays over your cash register.

Do have a vase containing three stalks of prosperity bamboo behind your cash register.

Do keep the counters near your cash register free of clutter, knickknacks, old receipts, phone books, and so on to facilitate the flow of prosperity chi around it.

Do put a charity collection box near your cash register to create good karma for you *and* your customers, who will be sharing their abundance with those less fortunate.

Do tape a lai see (a red enve-
lope) to the bottom of your
cash register for money luck
(but not to the drawer, where it
could be easily seen or stolen).

147

Do place Chinese coins in the corners of your new home's foundations during its construction.

Do tape antique Chinese coins wrapped in red paper to the underside of your cash register, fax machine, computer, and/or telephone for increased money luck.

Do hang three Chinese coins with red ribbon or cord on the inside doorknob of the front entrance of your home or business.

Don't make the mistake of hanging any Chinese coins on your back door— or money will exit your home or business.

Do incorporate square and round shapes in your décor for financial success. Remember that ancient Chinese coins were round (heaven) with square (earth) holes at their centers.

Do tape three Chinese coins

tied together to an inside sec-

tion of your wallet so that it will

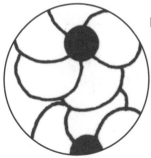

never be empty

of money.

Don't lose the coin that fits in your money frog's mouth. Secure it with glue so pets and children don't bump your wealth luck loose. (And be sure that your money frog is on the ground.)

Do create or wear jewelry crafted from Chinese coins to attract financial abundance.

Do notice that red (fortune) and green (prosperity) are popular color combinations for Chinese businesses, as are their varia-tions: peach and teal.

Do use more blue instead of

black to represent water—

black is too yin and is associated

with mourning.

COLOR

Do include the color red in your clothing (visible or hidden, such as lingerie). Notice that Tiger Woods always wears a red shirt on the last day of every tournament—it represents fame, celebrity, protection, and prosperity.

Do wear purple if you want to feel wise and wealthy, for it's the color of riches and royalty.

Don't add any shades of red to the metal areas of W and NW.

Do add purple to the S

and SE for wealth and

material

abun-

dance.

Do use green, blue, and black

in the E and SE—it will bring

water to the element of wood.

Do use lighter

colors for

your ceilings

to bring more

yang energy into your business.

Don't have black-colored ceilings.

Do use lots of earth colors (such as yellow) in a home bathroom that extends past the front door.

Don't have a clock radio with red numbers on the nightstand next to your bed, for it will generate much nega-tive, electromagnetic energy, the equivalent of sha chi.

Do invest in a liquid-filled hiking compass for use in properly designing your home or workplace according to classical feng shui.

Do choose your natural crystals by feel or the emotions they evoke when you hold them in your hand.

Don't let other people touch or handle your crystals (especially the ones you use for healing and cleansing energy).

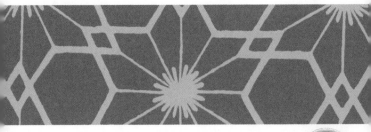

Do put the power of

natural and cut crystals

to work for your

financial success.

Don't move your crystals after you notice an increase in business. Keep them clean and in the same place.

Do disperse negative sha chi—from rooflines, lampposts, gables, building corners, and so forth, visible through windows—with a crystal cluster on the sill.

Do have a piece of black tourmaline in your pocket to keep you feeling grounded, especially if you're working around a lot of electronic or technical equipment.

Do keep your natural

crystals activated by

recharging them in

the moonlight.

Do place a heavy quartz crystal

or ball on the outside corner of

your desk to anchor good fortune.

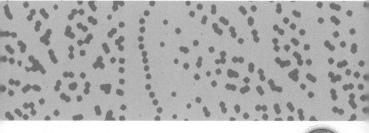

Do keep your citrine (money) and amethyst crystals in the earth (NE, SW) and metal (W, NW) areas of your office.

Do cleanse the energy of your

gemstone jewelry or crystals

after wearing or using them by

giving them a saltwater bath

and air-drying them with their

points facing down.

Do face the main entrance of a room (but not directly in line with it) while sitting at your desk because this shows that you're welcoming business as it approaches.

Don't choose a desk that faces an escalator, elevator, or stairs.

Don't sit with your desk directly in line with the office's entrance door, as it will adversely affect your health with "rushing" energy.

Do have a desk custommade for you with the auspicious feng shui dimensions of 35" (89 cm.) wide by 60" (152 cm.) long by 33" (84 cm.) high, and watch your business skyrocket!

Don't position your desk so that your back is to a window unless there's a mountain or building (symbolic mountain) outside to provide support; instead, sit with your back to a wall.

Do place a picture of a mountain, a stone or ceramic statue or figurine, or a crystal geode on the sill if you sit at a desk with a window behind you.

Don't choose a desk that's located behind a door.

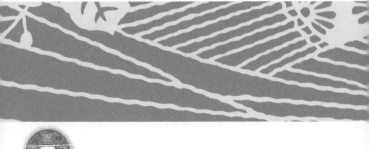

Do keep your desk from your first, prosperous business, for it possesses auspicious energy.

Do keep your desk free of clutter to facilitate prosperity energy. Be brutal with everything that comes across your desk—act on it, stow it, or toss it.

Do match the various elements of the items on your desk with their compass directions.

Don't place more than nine extraneous objects on your desk (and be sure that the items correspond to the bagua map).

Do break up killing sha energy

with a faceted crystal ball or

jar on your desk.

189

Do position a statue or figurine of a pig or boar on the outside corner of your desk to activate your money luck.

Do have a figurine of a rat

sitting on a mound of gold

coins on your

desk for abun-

dance.

Do put a statue of a deer on your desk to symbolize prosperity and long life.

Do place a wish-

fulfilling cow on the

outside corner of

your desk.

Don't crowd the wealth-attracting

animals—or your desk will

resemble a miniature zoo!

Do hang

artwork

of the

double carp in

your dining room.

Do keep a tabletop fountain in the dining room of your home.

Do choose the seat diagonally across from the door to the conference room for meetings, as this is the power/command position.

Do use only one

door in your office—

if there are more,

keep them closed.

Do use tiger statues facing away from each other on either side of your office door for protection.

Do keep an aquarium or fish tank near the front door of your store to attract lots of money luck, just like your favorite Chinese restaurant does!

Do place a three-legged prosperity frog on the floor next to your front door, facing in with a coin in its mouth—this means money will be carried into your home.

Do position a standing elephant on each side of your home's main entrance as guardians for your home.

Do trim back overgrown bushes and hedges that extend their foliage into the path to your front door.

Don't install any water elements, such as a pond, waterfall, or fountain, on the right side (as you look out) of your front door. Water is yin (female), so to add it is to bring the influence of another female into your household.

Do add blue, black, and green accessories into your home or office décor—especially to the wood areas of E and SE, both of which represent good fortune.

Do use images

of dragons on

an E or SE

wall for

prosperity.

Don't put any metal items in the E or SE wood areas because metal destroys prosperity and harmony.

Do add a carved wooden turtle to the E for harmony and protection in your workplace.

Do add wood furniture and other items to the E and SE areas of your home to increase money luck.

Do avoid using fans as wall decorations in your business because the Chinese word for *fan* is also a homonym for *scatter*.

Don't toss away feathers that you find near your home—tie them together and place them by your front door for protection.

Don't buy bird feathers for decorations inside your home or office.

Don't ask for

feathers from

other people.

Do acquire the furniture of a successful or expanding business.

Don't purchase furniture from a bankrupt business (no matter how good a deal you get), as it can carry negative energy that will negatively affect *your* business.

Don't sell or give away office furniture from your first successful business; instead, keep these good-fortune "charms" in your possession.

Do use wood furniture with

carved dragons in its design for

power, strength,

and vitality.

Do use two metal crane waterspouts in the N area of your garden.

Don't place a statue

of a deity directly

on the ground

outdoors.

Do place a pair
of metal cranes
in the N part of
your garden.

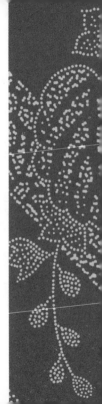

Don't set your altar

on the ground

in your garden

or patio.

Do give potted kumquat or orange trees as gifts of prosperity to a new business.

Don't present a business with miniature plants such as roses or a bonsai tree, as these represent limited growth rather than expansion.

Do bestow a money tree with leaves crafted from semiprecious stones to a business on opening day.

Do give a

statuette of a

Chinese unicorn

to bring good

luck to a new business.

Do bestow the gift of a succulent jade plant with its rounded, plump leaves as wishes for promotion and business success.

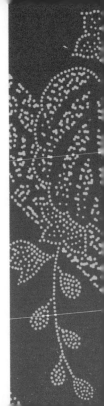

Do remember that feng shui's origin was for the proper placement of ancestors' graves—and finding ideal sites was the ultimate show of honor and respect. So find the best possible gravesite for your loved ones . . . and it will also ensure *your* good fortune.

Don't choose a gravesite for a loved one near a curb or within the sound of vehicular traffic.

Do always keep your parents' and ancestors' gravesites tidy and clean.

Do cleanse the energy in your home and work-place several times a year by smudging, ringing bells, clapping, or other methods.

Don't buy a home that's located at the end of a cul-de-sac, as it will absorb the killing sha energy from the cars and road directed toward it. Rule of thumb: Any building that a car's headlights hit is receiving killing sha energy.

Do decorate with dragon

designs to improve harmony

in your home and bring

more yang

energy in.

232

Don't use funeral images such as statues or masks as home accessories, for they contain dark yin energy.

Do keep all metal

exercise equipment

out of the E part of

your house or bed-

room because metal

destroys good health.

Do buy a home that has its kitchen stove against a wall, which represents support for the family's money luck.

Don't choose a house that has a kitchen with a stove located on a peninsula or an island—there's no support behind the household's wealth.

Do keep your stove or oven clean and in excellent working order, as they represent the family's prosperity.

Don't put your fish tank or aquarium in your kitchen because water puts out the fire (long life and prosperity) element there.

Don't display your kitchen knives in plain sight—this encourages disharmony in the household.

Do try to face E (wood) or S (fire) when you cook.

Don't have the stove and sink on the same counter because water puts out fire (fortune).

Don't locate a sink and a stove directly across from each other in your kitchen, as this causes quarreling.

Do use the horse as a part of your logo if your business is in the field of flight, travel, trade, or transportation.

Do use a mirror to deflect the killing sha energy originat-ing from power lines, lamp-posts, and tree trunks.

Don't hang the traditional bagua mirror (a round mirror with red, green, and gold surrounding it) anywhere inside your home.

245

Do use a bagua mirror to deflect the negative energy of unpleasant neighbors. Don't be surprised if they move away as they get "a taste of their own medicine"!

Do install a flat, round mirror facing your backyard swimming pool if it's located in the S part of your property.

Don't set up a bagua mirror so that it faces a school, road, office building, or other occupied structure.

248

Do install a small round or octagon mirror, facing out, above an enclosed toilet's door frame if it's located in the SE (material abundance) area of your home.

Do use a round compact or other ordinary mirror to deflect unsightly views from your windows.

Do keep a

single black

box in the N.

Do place a crystal turtle, symbolizing riches, in the N part of a room.

Do put your computer in the N area of your office to develop new business and communications.

Do have a laundry room in the N part of your house or condo. The element of water represents cleansing.

Do keep a bubbling tabletop fountain in the N area of your office, workspace, or desk to activate business success.

Do situate your fish tank or aquarium in the N part of your office to stimulate business and career growth.

Do place a metal or ceramic turtle in a bowl set in the N for prosperity.

Do improve your focus and direction with a quartz crystal in the NE of your workspace.

Do hang your

certificates,

diplomas, and

so forth in the NE area of

your office.

Do use a grouping of eight natural crystals in the NE of your home or office to improve your self-development and wisdom.

Do add pyramids to stimulate the earth areas of knowledge (NE).

Don't put candles in the NW sector or it will keep helpful people away.

Do bring in porcelain and

china accessories to

the NW to stimu-

late trade and

travel.

Don't remove trees in the NW part of your property, as they represent fatherhood and support for your household.

264

Do place six citrine, quartz, or amethyst balls in the NW of your home or workplace to shore up the benevolent power of the male head of the family or business.

Do use the power of the citrine (wealth) in the NW area of your office.

266

Do put a coin bank in the shape of a pig in the NW or W part of your child's room.

Do pick an office with auspicious numbers such as one, three, six, eight, nine, or combinations of these.

Don't use a group of five horses

for decoration, as this is unlucky.

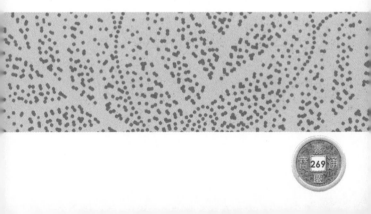

Do group eight crystals in the NE to enhance your personal growth and development.

Don't use antique Chinese coins in multiples of five—only in threes, sixes, and nines.

Do add live green plants in multiples of three if there's disharmony and friction in your workplace.

Do put dragon

statues together

in groupings

of two, three,

or nine.

Do have your

new office, store,

or home blessed

before you

move in.

Do choose an

office (or home)

that has a square

or rectangular footprint so that

it's balanced and "complete."

Don't pick an office building that has a road aimed directly toward it, as this represents sha chi, or killing energy.

Don't select the tallest building on your block for your office site. Like the World Trade Center, it will be the most vulnerable, as it lacks protection.

Do avoid hiring negative or critical people in your workplace, since their negative energy will encroach upon yours.

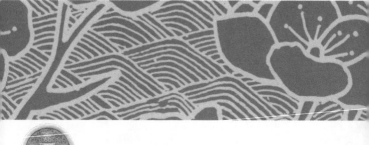

Do keep company with success-ful, affluent people, for you'll benefit from their wealth energy.

Don't rent or lease an office that you have to walk down to (such as a basement).

Do remove

as much

clutter as you

can from your office.

Don't use candles in your office, as they "burn" prosperous wood energy.

Do ring a brass handbell for

cleansing the energy

in your office after

a meeting.

283

Do balance your office with yang energy by using a dragon motif.

Don't decorate your office with accessories that have funeral connotations, as they're bad luck.

Do hang Chinese scrolls with
the calligraphy of good fortune
in your office.

Don't have more than one entrance into your office. Use a single door to direct your energy and wealth inside.

Don't introduce symbols of love and romance into your workplace— these should only be placed in your home.

Don't occupy

any office that

has a view of

the rest rooms.

Do put up a freshwater turtle shell for protection in your building.

Don't place your company's eating or food-preparation area next to or across from the rest rooms.

Do hang pictures of swimming

terrapins behind you at

your workplace.

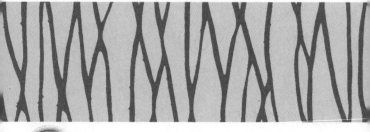

Don't leave your

cleaning tools in

sight at your

business.

Do place a statue of an

elephant with its trunk curved

upwards (which is a symbol of

strength and wisdom)

in your office.

Do increase the yang energy in an office or room by adding the image of a standing or galloping (not rearing) horse.

Don't position your work surface so that you're literally turning your back on business coming through the door.

Do include a painting or other artwork of a flock of wild geese flying "into" your office to represent good news coming.

Do hang a painting
of deer in your office
for wealth and riches.

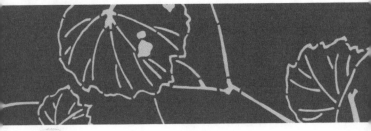

Do accessorize your workplace with a pair of crane statues for long life.

Do honor your

departed loved ones

with remembrances,

photos, and mementos

tucked away in quiet

corners of your home.

Don't place photographs
of deceased relatives
on the wall
above your
fish tank or
aquarium.

Do display paintings of cardinals for longevity.

Don't hang dragon pictures too high up on a wall.

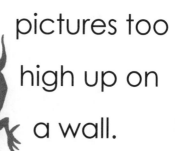

Do exhibit pictures of nature

around your workplace if your

business deals with technology.

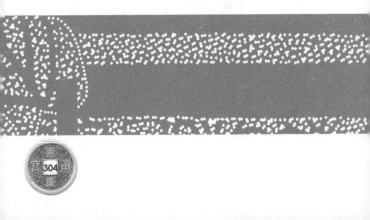

Do decorate your home or office with a model sailing ship loaded with miniature gold coins or mounds of semi-precious stones. And make sure to face the ship inward to symbolize prosperity entering your home or business.

Do bring in a
balance—
in the form
of live,
rooted plants—if your office
has a preponderance of
technical, medical, or
scientific equipment.

Do keep living water plants (such as prosperity bamboo) next to your cash box or register.

Do make your own money tree

by hanging Chinese coins with

red cord on the branches

of an indoor plant.

Do remove any indoor plants such as cacti that have thorns, spikes, or barbs, for these generate mini-arrows of killing sha energy.

Do decorate with a happy

Buddha at your business—

put him up on a high

shelf facing the

main

entrance.

Don't put a three-legged money frog on a high shelf.

Do locate any religious statues on a shelf that's higher than the tallest person.

Do decorate with red candles in the S for fame and fortune.

Don't add turtle figurines or art-work to the S. Turtles repre-sent water, thus putting out the element of fire, which symbolizes fortune.

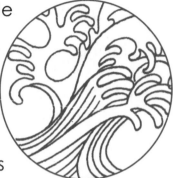

Do keep gifts from, and photos with, celebrities in the S part of your desk or office.

Do decorate with red birds in the S for happiness and joy.

Do use red and purple in the S to stimulate celebrity, awards, and fortune.

Do display your awards
and trophies in the S
area of your office.

Do hang a photo-graph of a soaring eagle on the S or SW wall in your office to uplift your business potential.

Do use images of the

phoenix on an S wall for

prosperity.

Do face a horse statue toward the S because it's one of the most yang directions.

Do hang a round, flat round mirror above a bathroom door's frame if it's in the SE prosperity area of a house.

Do put your computer in the SE part of your desk or office if the work you do on it generates income.

323

Do place a turtle carving in the SE to enhance material abundance.

Do multiply your abundance by locating your copy machine or printer in the SE area of your office or business.

Do decorate with two smoky or clear quartz balls in the SW area of your home or office to support the female head of the household.

326

Do fill a porcelain or ceramic vase with semi-precious stones or

crystals for wealth and place it in the SW.

Do put a pyramid shape in the relationship area of SW to stimulate strong rapport and support within your company.

Do hang a wind chime in an SW bath-room or toilet.

Don't sit at a conference table with your back to the door, as this weakens your influence.

Do use a round or oval

conference table.

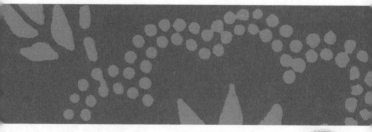

Do carry a piece of jade, coral,

or black onyx in your pants

pocket if you're

a traveling

businessperson.

Do cleanse the energy in your hotel rooms by smudging, ringing bells, clapping, airing, or other methods.

Do cover up your hotel room's dresser mirror with a bath towel if it reflects any part of your body on the bed.

Do don a pendant or piece of jewelry made of your birth-stone, jade, or coral for protection when you travel if you're a woman.

Do wear the color red, either
visible or as underwear, to keep
you safe when you take trips.

Do maintain the trees and other flora on your property for continued good money luck.

Do remove any diseased or dead trees, hedges, or bushes, for they generate negative sha energy toward your home.

Don't cut down any mature trees if they're located in NW, as this is the area of helpful people and trade.

Do thin out and shape your trees to minimize too much shade (yin) and to allow sunlight and breezes to come through.

Don't plant a tree so that its trunk is directly in front of your door. This obstructs the beneficial chi from entering as well as the owner's perspective of the world when looking out.

Do try to include pine, bamboo, magnolia, peach, plum, or gingko trees on your property, as these represent good luck and fortune.

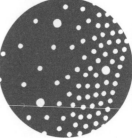

Do include evergreen plants in your landscaping—minimize deciduous ones because they'll generate sha chi when the dead leaves drop around your home.

Do construct a waterfall that faces toward an exterior door or window leading to the dining room of your home. Keep it open as much as possible to encourage prosperity chi to enter.

Do create a balance of yin energy (water, shade) with yang energy (rocks, sun) in your garden or pond.

345

Don't paint your ceilings black, even though it symbolizes water (business, career). It's too yin and will actually mean that you're "underwater." Use a medium shade of gray (which represents metal or coin) instead.

Do hang artwork of tortoises or turtles swimming in water for good money luck.

Do have clean running water such as a creek or stream in front of your property, as this symbolizes wealth flowing to you.

Don't face dragon statues toward water outside your building.

Do put a moving

water element in

the N, E, or SE area

of your office.

Do use natural materials

when constructing your

pond.

Do stimulate creativity with

artwork depicting a walking (but

not attacking) tiger in the W.

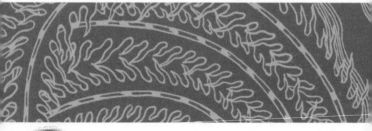

Do add earth materials such as clay and terra-cotta to the W to spike your creativity.

Do avoid using candles in the W, as this is a metal area of imagination.

Do place a piggy bank

filled with silver coins in

the W or NW area of

a home.

Do keep your deposit slips in the W part of your desk or office to symbolize your harvesting the fruits of your labor.

Do raise the power of your concentration by activating the energy of a white quartz crystal in the sunlight of the W.

Do use the shapes of squares (earth), arches, semicircles, and circles in the W to enhance metal and money.

Do add metal sculptures and other items in the W and NW to enhance creativity and helpers in your life.

Do use hollow-rod wind chimes to draw up or activate stagnant energy.

Do choose your wind chimes for their tones (which should be light and tinkling) to generate yang energy.

Do hang wind chimes to match or support the elements of the compass directions: wood or bamboo for E, SE, and S; metal for W, NW, and N; ceramic for NE and SW.

Don't install any

wind chimes

over your bed

or desk.

Do place wind chimes where a breeze will make  them sound yet won't disturb your neighbors (which would create bad karma).

Do use wind chimes to enlarge

your network of friends, donors,

mentors, and supporters.

ZODIAC

Figure G – The Chinese Zodiac is based on a 12-year cycle, and each year is represented by an animal. Find the year you were born to determine your sign.

Pig (born in 1935, 1947, 1959, 1971, 1983, or 1995):
You're a good companion who makes lifelong friends—an intellectual who needs to set difficult goals and carry them out. You're sincere and tolerant but tend to be naive. Be careful: Your headlong quest for material goods could be your downfall.

Dog (born in 1934, 1946, 1958, 1970, 1982, or 1994):
You're an honest and reliable person, faithful and loyal to those you love. You work well with others, but a sharp tongue and fault-finding can cause problems. You worry needlessly and can be stubborn.

Rooster (born in 1933, 1945, 1957, 1969, 1981, or 1993):
You're very intelligent and know how to influence people. A hard worker, you're shrewd and decisive and should achieve your goals. When you speak your mind, you may seem boastful. Extravagance is a problem.

Monkey (born in 1932, 1944, 1956, 1968, 1980, or 1992):
You're clever, with a magnetic personality that makes you well liked. Your pioneering spirit and quest for knowledge makes you an ardent worker. You may be considered eccentric by some. Guard against distrust of others.

Goat (born in 1931, 1943, 1955, 1967, 1979, or 1991):
You're creative and artistic but tend to be timid. Try not to get off on the wrong foot with people, as you can be charming company. Avoid a pessimistic outlook, and don't count on material things to make you happy.

ZODIAC

Horse (born in 1930, 1942, 1954, 1966, 1978, or 1990):
You're a friendly and popular person, attractive to the opposite sex.
You have a capacity for hard work and can be very independent.
You're often ostentatious and inclined to be egotistical.

Rat (born in 1936, 1948, 1960, 1972, 1984, or 1996):
A generous free-spending charmer, you make no lasting
friendships. You're honest and imaginative, but your ambitions
make you seem like an opportunist. Watch your temper, and
don't be overly critical of others.

Cow (born in 1937, 1949, 1961, 1973, 1985, or 1997):
You're a born leader. While you're happy alone, your patience
would make you a good parent. You're conservative and
methodical, but you like to have your own way. You're very
good with your hands.

Tiger (born in 1938, 1950, 1962, 1974, 1986, or 1998):
You're courageous and aggressive, to the point of getting carried
away. You can be very stubborn. You have strong emotions and
are capable of great love.

Rabbit (born in 1939, 1951, 1963, 1975, 1987, or 1999):
You're an articulate and talented person—a peace seeker. You're obliging
and pleasant, affectionate, and usually very lucky. Your conservative and
cautious nature is an advantage.

Dragon (born in 1940, 1952, 1964, 1976, 1988, or 2000):
You have a passionate nature, full of vitality and enthusiasm. You're gifted and intelligent
and strive for perfection—demanding the same of others. You have good health and
great popularity.

Snake (born in 1941, 1953, 1965, 1977, 1987, or 2001):
You're very charming and romantic, a deep thinker who's strongly intuitive. Your
physical attractiveness tends to make you vain. Avoid stinginess, don't procras-
tinate, and never lose your sense of humor.

Do consult the Chinese zodiac compatibility chart when choosing employees or partners.

Do hire an employee born in the Year of the Dog for loyalty.

Do decorate with the image of hares if you were born in the Year of the Rabbit.

Do use logos and art depicting the ram if you were born in the Year of the Goat.

Do display the auspicious statue of a rat on a pile of Chinese coins if you were born in the Year of the Rat to increase your resourcefulness and intuition.

Do wear a pendant with the Chinese character for "snake" if you were born in the Year of the Snake to increase your business savvy.

Do decorate with images of dogs if you were born in the Year of the Dog to stimulate your insightful- ness, and loyalty in your employees.

Do surround yourself

with dragon designs,

furniture, art, and clothing

if you were born in the

Year of the Dragon.

Do display artwork depicting horses gallop-ing or standing with their heads up in dignity if you were born in the Year of the Horse.

Do use art with images of monkeys

if you were born in the Year of

the Monkey to spike up your

cleverness in financial

matters.

377

Do place a statue of a cow atop Chinese coins at the corner of your desk if you were born in the Year of the Cow to increase your logical thinking and steadfastness.

Do fill a ceramic piggy bank and place it in the SW if you were born in the Year of the Pig.

Do put a painting of a resting or strolling tiger on a W, NW, or N wall if you were born in the Year of the Tiger.

Do accessorize with images or figures of a rooster (and a hen) if you were born in the Year of the Rooster.

Angi Ma Wong is an internationally recognized feng shui expert/consultant and the bestselling author of *Feng Shui Dos & Taboos*. She has appeared on *Oprah*, *Regis & Kelly*, CNN, *CBS Sunday Morning*, the Discovery Channel, and in *Time* magazine. Website: **www.FengShuiLady.com**